# Star of Free Will

Essential Poets Series  63

# Maria Luisa Spaziani

# Star of Free Will

*Translated by Carol Lettieri*
*and Irene Marchegiani Jones*

Guernica
Toronto / New York
1996

Original Title:

*La stella del libero arbitrio*

The original work was published by Arnoldo Mondadori Editore in 1986.

Copyright © Maria Luisa Spaziani, 1986.

Translation © Carol Lettieri, Irene Marchegiani Jones and Guernica Editions Inc., 1996.

Antonio D'Alfonso, Editor.

Guernica Editions Inc.

P. O. Box 117, Station P, Toronto (Ontario), Canada M5S 2S6

340 Nagel Drive, Cheektowaga, N.Y. 14225-4731 U.S.A.

Typesetting by Jean Yves Collette.

Printed in Canada.


This publication was assisted by the Minister of Foreign Affairs (Government of Italy)
through the Istituto Italiano di Cultura in Toronto (Director: Francesca Valente)
and Vancouver (Director: Gabriella Bianco).


Legal Deposit — Fourth Quarter

National Library of Canada.

Library of Congress Catalog Card Number: 94-75325.


Canadian Cataloguing in Publication

Spaziani, Maria Luisa

Star of free will

(Essential poets ; 63)

Translation of: La stella del libero arbitrio.

ISBN 1-55071-002-8

I. Lettieri, Carol. II. Jones, Irene Marchegiani. III. Title. IV. Series.

PQ4879.P29S513 1994 851'.914 C93-090548-2

96 97 98 99 10 9 8 7 6 5 4 3 2 1

# Table of Contents

## Various Adventures

## The Cemetery at Prima Porta

## Viterbo Environs

## Poetry

## Diary from France

## Zodiacal Sunday

## Crisis

# Translators' Preface

In the poetry of Eugenio Montale, one of Italy's greatest twentieth century literary figures, Maria Luisa Spaziani appears as the Vixen – the poet's vital, animalistic muse. But despite their close literary and personal association, Spaziani has not contentedly relegated herself to the shadowy, traditionally feminine Other. Author of nine volumes of poetry and Italian translator of Racine, Shakespeare, and Marguerite Yourcenar (among other French, English, and German writers), Maria Luisa Spaziani has enjoyed a long, prolific and independently successful career. Her verse has been translated into numerous languages and has appeared in English in American anthologies. *Star of Free Will* marks her first book-length publication in English.

Born in Turin in 1924, Maria Luisa Spaziani has lived in Rome since 1957 and works in Sicily, where she has taught as Professor of French Language and Literature at the University of Messina since 1964. French literature, particularly the symbolist verse of Rimbaud, has been – as the poet herself avows – one of the primary influences upon her work. For Spaziani, Rimbaud's "*Bateau ivre*" epitomizes all of modern poetry: "this drunken boat. . . has lost its course, has lost everything, just like modern man. . . And if that weren't enough, this little poem that turns everything upside down. . . is written in regular, rhymed alexandrines." It is the paradoxical blend of formal control imposed on the irrational that fascinates Spaziani.

Spaziani made her debut on the Italian literary scene in *Quarta generazione*, a pivotal 1954 anthology introducing the "fourth generation" poets (Erba, Chiara, Orelli, Cattafi, Zanzotto, Luzi) who, in reacting against the post-war "neo-realists," returned to the hermetic tradition of Ungaretti, Montale, and Saba by reviving heightened poetic language, evocative imagery, and classical verse forms. But despite her initial association with these "neo-hermetic" poets, Spaziani resists categorization. In an obvious allusion to the turn-of-the-century *crepuscolari* ("twilight poets"), Spaziani writes:

> I loved lovers of twilight too,
> fishermen of shadows, the offended, the mortified.
> Admirable masters, they helped me
> to become their exact opposite.

She has in over three decades of literary output refused to be circumscribed by the many movements – from the avant-garde "*i novissimi*" of the 1960s to the feminists of the 1990s – that have characterized postmodern Italian poetry.

Though Spaziani at times experiments with language as the avant-garde poets did, she refuses experimentation for its own sake. Though in sympathy with Italian feminists, she, herself, has never felt constrained by her gender nor suffered from the "victimization complex" that she associates with many women writers. Indeed, Spaziani told us in an interview in Rome in the summer of 1992: "In my life, I have always proceeded like a man."

At age thirty, Spaziani sent out her first collection of poetry to the prestigious Mondadori publishing house – without accompanying letters or recommendations – and in eight months the manuscript, *Le acque del sabato* (1954), was published in the same "Specchio" series that had showcased the work of Montale, Saba, and Ungaretti. With each successive collection – *Il gong* (1962), *Utilità della memoria* (1966), *L'occhio del ciclone* (1970), *Transito con catene* (1977), *Geometria del disordine* (1981), *La stella del libero arbitrio* (1986), *Giovanna d'Arco* (1990) and her most recent *Torri di Vedetta* (1992) – she has carved out her own lyrical voice, often at odds with the style in vogue, be it political engagement, the deconstruction of the "I," fragmentation of language, or feminist protest.

For Spaziani, the lyric has always been primary. She privileges the poetic act over political engagement and maintains faith in the power of language to enrich and give meaning to contemporary experience. Using the standard hendecasyllable measure, she writes in the "high style," but her imagery is hard-edged and modern. As Luigi Baldacci has noted, she appropriates traditional forms only to confound them in the service of her own ends. Though lyrical, her vision is startlingly unromantic.

In *Star of Free Will*, Spaziani abandons traditional verse forms for a freer poetic line and introduces for the first time fragments of daily, conversational language into her poetry – juxtaposed against her typical "high" tone and striking metaphors. Spaziani seems more intent on speaking directly in this volume, and she incorporates more irony and humor into her poetic persona than in her previous works. But despite these departures, the shift is not radical: Spaziani remains true to the essential lyrical lines and thematic preoccupations that have characterized her work since its inception.

Like the titles of previous collections – *Transito con catene* (Transit in Chains), *Geometria del disordine* (Geometry of Disorder) – *La stella del libero arbitrio* (Star of Free Will ) embodies a paradox. How can a star – a fixed cosmic point, traditional symbol of predestination – be a beacon of free will? The image is an emblem for the contradictory nature of the reality that Spaziani embraces – and a metaphor for her own poetics. For in Spaziani's verse, formal control (the star) is wedded to imaginative explorations (free will).

The image of the star assumes various associations as Spaziani explores the nature of free will. In the title poem, "Star of Free Will," the star is identified with adventure, imagination, spontaneity:

> Dazzling adventure, last Muse of the West,
> coil released, genie lurking in human gestures,
> gentle, violent, lost, my errant flower,
> memorable star of all free will

But the star of free will is lost, an "errant flower" in the modern world.

> My brothers and children know little of you
> they're a trail of ants, flesh and gray suits in a bus,
> we wear the sixteen digits of our social security number
> branded on our chest like animals for slaughter –

Spaziani poses her poetic star against the monotony and depersonalization of life in a society that threatens to homogenize our behavior. But even when temporarily liberated from deadening routines, the poet realizes that freedom may only be a momentary illusion:

> This Sunday is over too;
> the calm will soon be broken.
> The will seems free. But for how long?
> The stars are pure fantasy.

The stars, as a symbol of transcendence and adventure, are a product of our own fancy. In a poem near the end of the collection, "To the Readers," Spaziani concludes that even for a poet the ideal union of star and free will is a myth:

> Free-will-star is a dream hendiadys,
> a pathetic longing, laughable today.
> Theory, utopia, hypothesis, folly.
> Neither I nor any star has ever been free.

Like the star that is fixed even though it appears to cross the sky, the poetic "I" is guided by unseen forces. Once the imagination is set in motion, metaphors are mysteriously transmitted to the writer.

> My star is a sea forging rhythms,
> reflecting caverns of a deeper yesterday.
> Metaphor is a veil hiding other mysteries.
> I can't see to its bottom. You are dictating to me.

Here the star evokes a poetic imagination that is not free but destined to haunt the past, opening psychological abysses over which the writer has no control.

In its coolness and detachment, the star is typical of the imagery that Spaziani employs. She focuses on the natural world and in deriving a substantial portion of her poetic discourse from the language of natural science, she uses the rational to speak of the irrational. And it is in this juncture that Spaziani becomes a postmodern poet, diagramming a disorderly and uncertain world through the use of orderly and self-possessed language.

Here also, Spaziani's classicism and modernity intersect. Classical allusions abound in the poetry, but even more importantly, Spaziani posits a "classical" persona in the contemporary world: The poetic "I" does not dissolve in the realization of its limits. The poet does not lose the measure and dignity of her eidetic memory. This classical control over emotions gives a curiously modern detachment to Spaziani's poetic voice – though it also places her, like many feminists, against those postmodern poets who favor a complete deconstruction of the subject. The strength of her poetic "I" pervades the poetry as a subject that becomes conscious of the boundaries of her freedom, the fragmentation of contemporary reality, and the limitations of reason – and in that very awareness she strengthens and reconstitutes herself.

In her belief that individual action, particularly artistic creation, creates meaning, Spaziani resembles the existentialists:

> If the world is without meaning,
> the real fault is yours.
> This ball of wax
> awaits your imprint.

Yet she differs by siding with the constitutive power of the word over direct political action:

> Absolutely no writing of poetry
> while one child is dying of hunger.
> You're wrong, Sartre: so many children die
> because the world knows nothing of poetry.

The motif of the journey – another classical and modern theme – is also used extensively. Spaziani links the idea of the journey to the adventurous spirit that she associates with free will. But these travels, originating in an external reality, become an interior journey, often down paths of memory that eventually lead back to their point of departure. Travel, like the poet's longing for open, cosmic spaces, expands the poet's interiority, and the terrain explored is formed and filtered by memory and experience of the past.

Composed as Spaziani was entering her 1960s, *Star of Free Will* evokes themes of aging and loss. One of the most haunting lyrical sections of the collection, "The Cemetery at Prima Porta," offers poems on the death of the poet's mother and a man, presumably a lover. Spaziani faces these experiences stoically, even ironically, transmuting them into a magical language, the fundamental substance of her verse.

> The notes of that still intact dialogue
> pierce the earth of the thirteenth Christmas.
> Two stars are below, not in the sky,
> For these human eyes, all is a charm.
> All have leaves, warmth, energy.
> The universe is Christmas, a death-life braid,
> snow only contemplated, with a lost violet.

In translating Spaziani's poetry, we have tried most of all to capture the quality of her imagery: its simplicity, directness, sharpness – an unusual mix of the rational and the sensory. Capturing the music of her verse, of course, has been more difficult, for Spaziani's poetic line is often metrically complex, accentuated by assonance, alliteration, and rhyme or off-rhyme. Here, we have preserved those techniques when they could be used successfully in English, but when privileging sound over sense made for an awkward English line, we have chosen not to do so.

The most difficult challenge, perhaps, was in finding equivalents for Spaziani's neologisms. In the poems where she invents words based on Italian suffixes and roots, we did so only when such coinages would be recognizable in English. As often is the case in the balancing act of translation, we hope that any "betrayals" we have committed to the literal text have helped us to more faithfully render the spirit of Maria Luisa Spaziani's poetry to an English-speaking audience.[1]

*Carol Lettieri*
*Irene Marchegiani Jones*

---

1. Some of the same concepts and interpretations of Spaziani's poetry have appeared in Irene Marchegiani Jones, "Maria Luisa Spaziani: metafore dell'ambiente e dello spazio," *Italian Culture*, IX, 1991.

*When I use words, it is to pray*
*that you hear the depth of my silence.*
*A language does not exist (or has been forgotten)*
*for what I have to tell you.*

*A clown beat on a drum.*
*From his heart came the music of angels.*
*He saw no more the bear*
*lunging at his side.*

# VARIOUS ADVENTURES

# The Arches

Medallions of leaves blare,
autumn sabres the sea.
Earth, aromatic urn where
the seed of the future germinates.

My life, an unfinished cathedral,
awaits the western arch.
It dreams of it, mysteriously sketching in the background,
knowing the arch is the master pillar of the past.

At night mason-angels brush by
the unfinished portico: they rustle
like memories in the North Wind,
behind a shroud of eyelid and the void.

Pained blood, tears and reverie
cement the stones. I can now
absolve and encircle the eastern arch
that built itself in laughter.

# The Comet

My love for him had waxen wings –
long wings that seemed eternal –
beating steadily in the sky, brushing past peaks,
with unnerving nerve, pointing sunward –

Melted, the wings now grow inside me,
lost, only now they become real,
and to reckless hearts I cry: *passion is a phantom
too intense to become flesh.*

Wandering, long-haired Halley's comets, omens,
disasters, portents that enflame and chill the blood,
no one dare behold, nor risk touching
clots of pure distance – mirages

# Destiny

That was when destiny took me by the hand
and said, from this moment your white existence
melts into me, assumes a form never before seen –
from this moment you apprehend the heavens' infinity.

Your life was a rebus to decipher,
now here is the key, one sun alone illuminates you,
look how the flowers colored
when I alone said – *open your eyes* –

Death is a radical rending of breath
but you can see the medallion's other side –
they told you, child, that God is in everything
and it was pure allegory, equal to poetry –

In a castle of fog you have been imprisoned
your mind bat blind –
now walk, rise, I say. I told this to Eurydice
before you, to Lazarus, to all bewitched springs.

## The Street Lamps

A frenzied April lays down the law to the dead,
in a dance ancestral roots quiver,
the boy my father once was greens again,
his broken spears risk the streets of time –

In vast petals of shawls,
those April deliriums seemed endless,
now you can count them backwards, extracting them
like a thirsty man the last drops –

April is the great summit, the hub
of the wheel at the amusement park. Boxes of pure
emptiness, air and illusion, the graveyards laugh.
Oh my dead ones, street lamps gone mad in the wind.

# *Duomo*

The Duomo was thirty years younger when I lived in Milan,
Valkyrie a mad March galloped,
a yearning sky of acquamarine
smiled at my eyes of few memories.

Young girl, the school oak tree
with thirty rings less clasped around her heart,
the Velasca tower shiny brand new,
reflecting sunsets from Papuan islands.

Like a candle the tongue of fire,
each level's spire held its saint.
With my eagle eyes, I saw them smiling,
their eyelids quivering and repeating yes.

Under three full moons revolving all at once
a meadow of narcissi where Rimbaud danced
flowered for me on the church grounds.
I had a few more haloes in March in Milan.

## The Palette Goes Wild

Let loose, the wind strikes autumn's gong,
spidery clouds clutch the leaves,
the pitch ensares the green, the palette goes wild,
predictions and almanacs shattered to hell,

your remote face is a blunt instrument –
yesterday, strange to think of it, the moon was golden –
But you're not a sign, you're the entire zodiac
stirring in a witch's cauldron black and white –

Harvests, red brigades of poppies
become sheer memory.   Terrors and trances
fade into the past, the two faces of the medallion.
Useless and dying, off goes the last *Vanessa Pulchra.*

## The Mime

My fingernail traces senseless words of snow
on the glass of absence: winter, the ultimate mime –
in little cages of vertebrae water birds scream,
lakes crystals chasms planets abstract moons

## Birches in Leningrad

dancing whirling on my feet the buds like gems
concentric nocturnal rings mazurkas of branches
helicoids lace miniscule lips butterflies
green confetti entangled in mirages of moon –

Cruel epiphanies and incredulous springs

## The Lost Footsteps

All the lost footsteps in the hospital necropolis
condense into clouds on the glass ceiling.
Antiseptic manger the bed racks sigh:
give us an ox and a donkey, a merciful look.

Little wagons of coal, the stretchers plunge
towards the burning jaws of some foundry.
Spirits, I cry, wake up! What portentous alcohol
has distilled the life from our bodies?

Once there were poplars, mirth and adventure,
and above us all a sky not made of glass.
Red blood ran through the world's veins,
and we died, yes. But we died alive.

## More and More Seldom

More and more seldom we hear the angels sing.
The world overflows with exorcisms: an engine mortifies them,
a jet lacerates their wings, our haste so pitiful
it breaks the big wave, the net in which they're caught.
They are nymphs at the sunset of the pagan era,
taking refuge in caves, in the woods,
so intimidated and hounded they hate their own splendor.
Let us not bar these messengers completely
from our senses, the door to our souls.
They strike us with treacherous embraces
between a howl and a shriek: a green breath of wind,
the crest of a cloud, an omen
or a few notes of a symphony in D.
Very discretely they request our attention.
No refusal for the wishes of those to death condemned.

## *The Rue*

For years every leaf was hemlock.
Then the archangel flew down. Over roofs,
the silver of all new slate.
Sugar of Christmas was the snow
over blue, singing parapets.
Memory lost all weight.
I was a goat in Arcadia, nibbling on
sprouts of rue that instantly regrew.

## Nocturnal Flash

For thirty years I have probed the depths of my sea:
anchors, pearls, rusty nails –
each ray is refracted into strange pyramids,
forests of ferns die, corals sprout.

In anger and peace I filter light and dark,
if the lighthouse blinks I blink swiftly.
I lie in wait so the fish of Grace
won't pass me by as I sleep.

# The Executioner

Greenery gone, the dead-broke oak
sends messages in code. With false caresses
the wind's crude hand strips off the lifeless leaves.
"Retire," it hisses. "Resign," it howls.
"Make room on the branches for the next generation."

I immediately recognize the same invisible hand
that expelled the whitest feathers from my nest.
Useless kindness. A slap is more honest.
Don't stand on ceremony
with one too weak to bear witness tomorrow.

## Profiles Emerge

A hundred sleeping statues lie inside me –
I don't need any Michelangelo –
I am the sculptor
I am the mountain –

profiles emerge –
sand erases them –
wind disperses them –
profiles re-emerge –

eyelids beat in the heart of stone
a heart beats – help me

# *Barcelona*

My heart is a Gaudi design,
coiling and rising to defy the Baroque,
surfaces born of conical forms
under stony forests of bamboo.

Paraboloid of basalt and lava,
my heart is an excavation in disorder –
hyperbolic carbonized sequoias
testing the sky with rhythms of the millenium –

Virtually infinite, time is slow,
The Unfinished Rondanini Pietà,
path of all possibility, ascending spires
cut by an invisible laser.

## *Short Exercise in Abstract Invective*

badseed wolfhungry, noxious chokeweed,
evildoer, puffed up bloodshedder,
seedylowlife, shattered sword,
witchy, stealthy, sorceress,
lemures, demoness, dragoness,

......

## *School Janitor F. or The Nature of Free Will*

He made no more effort to pay off his three hundred debts
than Devil Robert, last of the buccaneers,
wasted nerve in years of pirating.
But he found no treasure, the drama
was unknown to him:
he lacked the time, will, or imagination
to believe in treasures.
Perhaps they existed in some blind alley, a cave or magic spell,
in an idea, an escape, a face, a heresy.
Always in a corner forbidden by law.

# *Victory*

Death's eyes don't move. But
in statues red blood flows.
Their pupils are alive. In fact
they, too, are destined to die.

But Death is immobile. Well she knows
that with each success, each trembling kiss,
we step forward on a path
that invites no one.

But each kiss, each written page
is a victory over her. (We must thank
whoever invented that fable.)

# *Short Song*

No path deceives,
no presage lies.
Who has struggled with the angel
remains phosphorescent.

## On the Rhythm of the Rosary

Winter comes of gentle wolves.
Civilized mists descend.
Recycled faces. Ruins
concealed under blankets of wisteria.

*In deserted churches the holy water evaporates.*

Like Purcell's Dido, I spent years
in silence singing *"Remember me."*
Youth is a sweet spring
lost in the salt of the sea.

# *Distance*

How many carrions of cats seemed like water-lillies
swept up in the wave of the beautiful years.
Distance is a kind hand,
a rosy mist over treacherous forests.

This pain, this ulcer, this bad dead cat.
Perhaps another water-lilly is ready to bloom.
Don't trouble your soul: your river of flowers
could be the Capuchins' crypt.

## Old Photograph

I was that smile, that flash
of light in those almond-shaped eyes.
What year? What season? Who was I smiling at?
A breeze playing with wisps of jet-black hair.

How often have I thought that it's Etruscan blood
that flows red in my veins.
But something equally mysterious connects me tonight
to those eyes, to those wisps of hair, to that forgotten breeze.

## The Movie

The movie of my life has thirty thousand scenes:
at least seven were memorable,
at least five are destined to endure –

Have you ever seen something enduring
that's spoken of in the past tense?

## Memory's Impotence

In the smell of hay, the past is
stratified, a Céroli of you.
The innocent rapture, and remembering it,
remembering that you have remembered it.

Every year the scent changed,
little by little the odor vanished.
The more heroically the memory persisted,
the stronger it held on.

In the smell of hay, my mother still
journeys (and our hearts follow).
Into the immense hall of an odorless museum
life is transformed.

## A Young Teacher

Sensing my heart was bound with a triple lock,
a man who said abracadabra
and lifted the veil of mist that enveloped my eyes
the Alhambras offered to the few,
the paradise denied to all others –

he put the seven right books in my hands,
and added a word on the economy of time,
on God and love, those absurd fables.
And he died young on a bank of the Po,
with Plato clenched in his clawing hands.

Linden trees bloomed, willows lapped the water.
For two days he lay there, found by no one.
Never before had he wasted so many hours and minutes
without thinking or writing, without listening to the
      [ linden trees.

## Flashes from an Italian Journey

The sweetest autumn comes.
In Capri hunters fire at each other.

*

With Magritte I saw an immense angel feather
supporting the Leaning Tower of Pisa.

*

A rose quickly aged, the Colosseum
has no will to bloom.

*

In heaven, bridges, *campielli,* and *calli* made of air.
Here where the water is heavier, we train.

*

Fabulous years blackmail me,
Vanilla and truffles, Monviso and my loves.
I, a good Ulysses with my ears closed.

*

The mockery of the goldfish, that memorable quiver
in the holy water stoup of Monza Cathedral.

*

Trulli in the Itria Valley: silhouette
of a Ku-Klux-Klan meeting.

## Candor

The innocent one who exists
without ever knowing of her existence –
in vain the red ray of remorse
wounds her.

Rising like a lilly,
taut and full of sap,
the dome of sky – a lake –
supporting its own weight.

A very strange day will come, indeed it will –
a day of hornets and fallen petals.
Why she was created, scripted and killed
will remain top secret in *saecula saeculorum.*

## Point Zero

Life turned pale,
a violet knowing nothing of a second bloom.
At times a thorn would emerge
pathetically to prick the sun.

Point zero has struck in the sky,
no gong could have announced it.
Like the dead awakening elsewhere,
the medallion welcomes us to its other side.

We will have the expanse of milleniums
to tally our first balance sheet.
All the radiance and evil
accumulated in a banal quarter of an hour.

## Proverbs Reconsidered

*Provence*

Clairvoyance doesn't come in a flash of lightning.

Don't set the woods on fire to warm a wayfarer.

*Western Ireland*

The blood of a lamb flows in your veins –
every wolf is on to your scent.

*Touraine*

Desperate to be happy, the poet
calls on the Huns to burn down his home.

*Sicily*

Carve promises of love in ice.
Place it in sunlight and wait for me.

*Arabia*

Intelligence is the thread that crosses
the warp of our strongest feelings.
If either one is missing, don't expect
a flying carpet.

The fool and his money
are quickly separated.
Leaving, the fool
loses his wings in flight.
Every pretext is useless
for redeeming the soul.
Every road that counts
must be traversed alone.

## Three Times

Precious sounds cascading, slithering eel,
message more perplexing than Sybil's oracle,

such a struggle to understand you, to decipher
a rigid filigree of words on a shroud of leaves –

Three times you trapped me, three times I escaped,
love, castle of fog, home of the Holy Grail.

# Star of Free Will

Dazzling adventure, last Muse of the West,
coil released, genie lurking in human gestures,
gentle, violent, lost, my errant flower,
memorable star of all free will –

My brothers and children know little of you,
they're a trail of ants, flesh and gray suits in a bus,
we wear the sixteen digits of our social security number
branded on our chest like animals for slaughter –

In a dream someone discovers you; you're a mystic rose
whose scent and form transcend the limits of cobalt blue,
the red blood of a thousand Tamerlanes,
the hippogriff pointing towards unsettling moons –

Every trail, every ocean, every sky, every mind
is striated with barbed wire, with prohibitions –
we are all Gulliver tied down with rules and ropes,
amidst the lilliputians impossible to break free.

# *Mango*

And the older I grow the more the secret name
from the lymph of my twenties is revealed.
Before it was a dark rhombus, a hieroglyphic
difficult to decode.

The name: I lay in wait for it. Four syllables
lilting, turning azure, a fresh mango.
I taste it on my lips, even though the sea
has swallowed up the fruit.

## When the Curtains Are Drawn

When I loved you I dreamed your dreams.
I watched your eyelids while you slept,
your eyelashes a light flutter.

                    Sometimes
wonder unfolds
– with unknown actors and lights –
when the curtains are drawn

# *Island of Salina*

Honeysuckle, wisteria, poppy,
dyer's broom, eucalyptus, caper,
medlar, orange blossom, vine:
triple trinity of the Peloritani Mountains
among obsidian shards coarse with brine.

Strange motionless existence that creates sparks.
Together we will lay down solid roots
within the blue of the northeast wind.

## Ship to Australia

Tiny seagull on the ship that resembles him
(a dot on the keel)
for the emigrants it's only a handkerchief,
another long wave goodbye.

In their eyes, the waving will go on
for years: the pure white of longing
against a line of black shawls
in the earthly paradise of the receding shore.

## Climbing Vines

There are thousands of stars to see
with a pair of good eyes. As in the darkness of a church,
all the rest is a cloud of incense.

The rendezvous is where the Big Dipper bends
to the pointless North.

Every night I ascend to wait for you there
my eyes hot climbing vines.

## Optical Illusion

The pacing of a past that doesn't pass
– a past that won't pale –
its nocturnal steps resound in ultrasound,
spew blue lances and misshapen stars,
disarray labyrinthinan ravines
through silent Sirens' barbicans.

In the rear-view mirror I recognize you,
my absurd lost one.
Your hair has highlights of dawn – come,
come, it's just starting.

# The Miracle

Winter's long face draws near. The ginkgo,
the tall Chinese tree called "one hyndred shields"
rings its green coins
against the elm, bereft of leaves.

The pristine corolla of a jeering flower
stares at me:
scathing youth at the top of the wheel
for a brief moment suspended.

Would we be fundamentally redeemed
if this little boat of ours, swan
who left the summits behind,
were to one day with a sudden flutter of wing
arise again?

They say that Lazarus was sickly and
pale for decades. He could not
cast off his ancient shroud
to rise again and make the terrible ascent.

## The Grain of Sand

In a grain of sand, the desert's origin.
In a molecule of water, life's origin.
One tomorrow morrow morrow morrow morrow,
the rosary unstrung by billions of hands.

At night one tomorrow is welded to another tomorrow,
twenty-four hours to be born, unfold, and die –
to die young, unravished,
the odalisque, forgotten by the pasha,
quickly shrivels.

Ever narrower are the binoculars,
days after days that at the end return.
The lens barely passes over rivers comets and clouds,
banners, birds of paradise, bolts of lightning.

Seems the world has never known
of a tomorrow the twin digit of another tomorrow.
But a line of yesterdays scutched and leveled:
gray, hooded, unredeemed days
sent to the rettery.

## Pure Idea

Happiness, be gone. I now have another calling
in the world.
Like fingers, tearless clouds
ploughed the moon,
eyes fertile, the other five senses
all stunned and shivering,
scattered over a hill,
bleached tufts of mythical daisies –

and *mare,* pure idea of sea, green
circumference self-enclosed,
like God, referring to nothing
but rhyming with everything *(amare*-love, *odiare*-hate
*generare*-generate, *ammazzare*-assassinate, *creare*-create)
sea of bitter rhymes and miserly shores
pulled into a delirium of vacuous horizons –

brotherhood of nerves and roots,
faces drawn near in moon powder,
happiness, be gone, dark and deep
is the well that is the key

## Farewell to Adolescence

The merchant of sand
makes a futile try to steal into
the bed of love.

## Rorschach Blot

Full of comings and fraught with goings,
with bisons of clouds the sky passes by:
great Rorschach blot, sending us omens
that are hard to decode.

If, between joy and glory,
you see a rose bloom
or a wound fester, a rash –

Don't push the horoscopes ahead
nor force them backwards:
for there your problem lies.

# THE CEMETERY
# AT PRIMA PORTA

*To my mother and Aziz*

Two people who in life barely touched
now two lone petals emerge from my flower.

O frail clouds over the fence of pines,
music box of farewells, messages returned to sender.

The notes of that still intact dialogue
pierce the earth of the thirteenth Christmas.
Two stars are below, not in the sky.
For these human eyes, all is a charm.
All have leaves, warmth, energy.
The universe is Christmas, a death-life braid,
snow only contemplated, with a lost violet.

## To the Dead

For you, my gentle ghosts, saying *tomorrow,* saying *knife*
makes no echo, makes no sense.
Faces are framed in strange pyramids.
I touch the stones. The shiver now is only mine.

Whitewashed as Europe's profile, the cast-off myth
is the body and its warmth the tendons, the perfume.
We will have new senses, unimagined dimensions.
In nettles the spirit will become incarnate.

Has there ever been a more despairing theme,
so discouraging for the poet so daring for the genius?
All we can do is protect and console ourselves – to think
that for you this crackle of branches is Beethoven.

# Fall at Prima Porta

### I

Over that grave I snow immensely,
endless and deep is my caress –
I lose I weep all my petals blooming over
and over to enfold a name

### II

That chrysanthemum brought it all back,
fearing and not fearing it –
ball of yarn, promise of a long marriage –

there are places where the sun rises endlessly

### III

deafening entanglement of pine
a death-rattle entwined in music –
O disintegrating gravel of fall,
emaciated memory of what is

## *Wind Rose*

Look that unnerves and inspires my future,
mouth that incarnates and absolves my past,
you my utmost adverb of time,
stone and fragile leaf, angel and snake,
wind rose, turning point
of the still possible

## My Mother Visiting

Dead for a year, sometimes she still pays me a visit,
arousing spring with open arms –
pollen, incense and clouds fuse, dancing
with words entangled in my branches –

The green woodpecker wires messages.
My heart skips a beat and doesn't know it.

Dry branch, remember.
This, your damnation.

## By the Window Panes

It's the hour of the moon, its milky ray warns me
that my mother's pressing on the window panes,
    [ not the solar pigeon.
She comes bringing me words of pure silence
that make the dictionaries pale.

Her words are tennis balls,
a game that can't be played without a partner.
For sure.   But on moonlit nights, I stand by the window panes,
ready to play, to play.

So close so out of reach, star-like man,
nebulous mystery to be won backwards,
last flame of March's windy rose,
petal that won't fall, that dies with its root –

star, richer star, snarled comet
not signifying mangers but embodying directions,
hard rock of dreams where I carve
words, unique and vain, in dark waters reflected.

That love that was delirium and liturgy,
an exhausting leap on breathless paths,
race trapped between forests in flames –

Years, decades become shadow,
shadow so sly and malicious,
fierce enough to shoot arrows –

Listen, listen to me, listen to life!
(You must listen in order to hear)

## *Marching Orders*

An inner compass keeps pushing me in your direction
like the wall towards the climbing vine –

To put roses in the vases of fermented time
to strip away past haloes
to make it flesh again –

To know something of you
I will turn to my poetry

The season – that flaunts a lofty peacock tail,
green comets transcending the grave's enclosure –
is listening with you to my absurd words.

You who in dying made all the living
a shadow more shade than shadow.

On that resplendent body now passes
something resembling a starry water.
They were real hands, soft shoulders.
Already they are pure fable.

If ever I am shipwrecked,
if stars destine me to starless waters,
may those high billows
have the curve of his lips.

Histrionic light give me back his cloudy profile,
the tulip upright in the fractured jar.
Lodged in my throat is a chalk-white staff,
a voice, violet and emaciated,
that raves and pines for imprisoned music.

# The Curtain

So dense is the darkness of this November,
the sea despairs of other light, and groping,
the receptive ear soars to music
only imagined, impalpable, filling in
all the nothingness of hypotheses –

           forever shut,
your gaze has drawn the curtain
with you; there is no substitute,
no understudy to make us believe in
the rest of the story.

An icy Danish night
lashes us with gusts of wind.
In a raspy voice the ghost speaks. The soliloquy's
dense echo makes the reef shudder.

Injunctions, peremptory commands
whisper in a mouthless darkness.
*"Because I am no longer among the living,
you must find a way to avenge me."*
To the dead's orders, the living are bound.
Of invisible steel, their chains.

# VITERBO ENVIRONS

*I have dug a deep Etruscan well,*
*and now I drink the fresh water of shepherds.*
*Under Soracte Mountain, even the wine of Horace*
*goes down without an ounce of vigor.*

*So true — sometimes I'm made drunk*
*on the fresh water of shepherds.*
*Summertime: when sleep casts me to the still warm ground*
*and the moon is a ball of snow.*

## *Pagan*

The apple I pick off the branch, the dew I bite into,
isn't from the tree of knowledge.
Nor is the dew the dew of the Hesperides
that promised a hundred years of life and lilly skin.
This apple is just an apple, an apple and nothing more.
The tiller of soil has always known that.
And if he isn't Adam, as I alone know,
this dawn is too bright to disappoint me.

## Notarized

I took an inventory of my passions
but I don't want debits
nor even credits, to tell the truth –

No one, during this Indian summer
of blonde grapes swelling on the vine,
dare speak to me of liquidation.

## From *"The Laughing Willows"*

I

From the top of the hill I descended into the Inferno,
The city of Lucumones opened into celestial blue,
Etruria in handsome profile, maidens imprinted on the wind,
dances painted in air, lovers submerged –

if a hole were dug for wisteria in the new home
a smile from unknown lips would appear,
distant, fervid voices: wicks, buckles, urns,
the shiny, earthen contours of a crumbling amphora –

Cast by an artisan while Sappho was alive,
this broken fibula once clasped the fairest tresses,
but the poet left us her verses and not a trace of her face:
here lie heads, bodies, and not a shadow of a word –

from the top of the hill I hear the call
rising from the depths of time and space,
fraternal ghosts accompany me nightly
and, laughing sweetly, listen to my troubles.

II

Now that I no longer have lovers, I share my solitude
with clouds forever solitary (they mate and part),
with stars unfathomably remote from other stars,
with butterflies and reptiles without a fixed abode –

only now I have learned how to live, to choose
my perfect lovers from those who are centuries away.
I invite Horace for dinner by his Soracte Mountain
where only a poet could imagine snow –

sometimes, to prune mimosas, I call an Etruscan to my side
with faultless profile and an apostle's long hands,
at the gate, Charon's chariot arrives,
carved griffins and dolphins – and the pit of hell is far away.

# The Last Night at Soracte Mountain

## I

Beside the window of farewells,
the rosebush takes in a light breath.
Innocent, it knows nothing of the betrayal.
The house is for sale.

Roots cannot be transported.
Neither can the soul, perhaps.
Nine new buds are about to bloom,
red buds for the new owner.

## II

On the last night at the house,
the trunk of the fir-tree is pure silver.
Yet there is no moon, no moon.
From an inner force its scales shimmer.

Even Soracte seems pure silver.
Among the last lillies and the blooming nettles,
only I am opaque, a failed flower,
a phantom with valises.

## III

I happened to light the fireplace,
thinking of her in the cold of the grave.
I seem to light the stars too
to illuminate her wherever she may be.

And every day she reciprocates
with little gifts.
The robin who arrived last night
brings messages in code.

## IV

Anomalous vessels – these clouds
without anchor nor crew.
The poet extends metaphors far,
knowing they transport us elsewhere.

A hundred eyelids has the rose – we know that,
but can't say it after Rilke.
Yet I didn't know how much a hundred eyelids
could multiply the tears.

## V

Charon weighs the dead's souls
and tonight I can feel that weight too
bending down the new shoots of the hibiscus
she once planted.

Like Aeneas, I promised her
I would found anew the lost home.
Better to leave Penates and ashes
to the wind's mercy.

# POETRY

*Sub specie aeternitatis.*
*Sub specie nostrae aetatis.*

## Protest on Principle

Absolutely no writing of poetry
while one child is dying of hunger.
You're wrong, Sartre: so many children die
because the world knows nothing of poetry.

# *Glory*

in the wind they've sown their long phrases
– wavering like scarves in the wind –
many scarves the wind has randomly torn
and carried away in shapes of unraveling clouds –

always the poet scorifying words in the wind
– three thousand drones die so that one can touch the queen –
writing writing and not even dying will they know
if their page were marble or water –

useless for the writer to question,
in your eyes your horoscope or angel is set –
sometimes water thickens into marble
*and this is a paradise called by many names* –

you saw yourself a raft, you're a grand vessel,
you saw yourself a parasol, you're a beetle flying free,
you saw yourself a heavy stone, incapable of splendor
but you're silver, you're the pyramid's summit –
and the most precious marble can suddenly reveal
cracks fine as a strand of hair,
then all shatters, crumbles, and the monuments of pride
dissolve into whirlpools that swallow up your name

# The Oil Lamp

The poet with her crown of solitude
is an olive pressed in the mill.
If only one sacred lamp
could shine in the world thanks to this oil.

Today grandeur is measured in meters, centimeters.
Take care to give it another name.
Slow and ungraceful we descend
toward the long consuming logosphere.

We are embers of great fireworks,
scorifying, sizzling, clouding dust,
a trace – not incandescent for long –
of dying comets.

## The Motor

My dreams are mad relics
of drowned brigantines of gold.
Pure mucilage. Desire
wants to grasp them but can't.

Perhaps that is why poetry
is still the motor of the mind:
the art of combining each memory
into a coherent dream.

## *Awaits Your Imprint*

Indifference is hell without flames.
Remember this when choosing,
between a thousand shades, your fatal gray.

If the world is without meaning,
the real fault is yours.
This ball of wax
awaits your imprint.

## Literary Survival

Death lies in wait at every word,
choosing each one with an infallible eye.
Equally infallible the archangel
takes the remaining words, stuffs them in a small bag
and aims straight toward the sky.

Never have they had
a fight.

## The Pretext

Poetry is the furrow that opens up between breakers,
a trench of paradise towards the promised land.
But if on the way you betray the mandate
a hundred walls of water will come roaring over you.

Its face, its step: a luminous pretext
between the inert world and a fire only mine.
The beloved is the real mediator
between sex and God.

## To Montale

You vanish, then herald yourself in other forms,
falsetto of wisdom in a playful mist,
ancient adolescent palm, trembling,
a flat note over strange waters.

Your disappearance is scandalous, a message
that disturbs internal meridians,
engages the future and drags along
pittosporums, tempests, and termitaries.

Will your footsteps disappear before
those who inherited your inacessible secrets?
The best part of the squid is the bone.
The rest is for the cooks.

## *Monterosso*

Intelligence is a salt (many have written this).
It counters the sugars of the heart, squeezes the orange
of the mind: word of the one who did not live in vain.
Intelligence alone teaches the right way to love.
Perhaps because love is intelligence.

The boats rotting in the shade of the small port
will never go to sea. The bard of Arsenio saw them
when he was young, without knowing he saw them.
For him our eyes caress the broken boards,
the torn flags of many fights with the angel.

Intelligence chooses in its darkness. Then in sun
it filters and synthesizes, airing its results.
Where the tap-root reaches is better unasked.
Don't challenge the secret source where light germinates.

# Epigraph for Montale

Wayfarer illuminated among many marching shades.
All you have lost by dying is your mortality.

# DIARY FROM FRANCE

## I

Pigeons take me for a French queen;
they alight on my marble scarf.
Sometimes they soil it: irrefutable proof
of their good faith.

All animals love me in Paris.
And this love is returned. No offense to men.
But those creatures didn't storm the Bastille
and find a thousand subtle ways to be forgiven.

## II

In Saint-Germain the rain falls gray on the pavement,
but here on the mansard roof it swirls blue.
Drenched, the Dove of the Holy Spirit
lands on the temple's lightning-rod.

For the tenth time – ten rotund moons –
I come like a peasant to filter essences.
Then I carry them away to dissolve them in Southern waters.
Like Jan the alchemist who compelled youth.

## III

I read three hundred books at the *Nationale,*
journals and incunabula, manuscripts and their variants.
But more numerous were my own inventions
in the small adjacent garden called "Four Rivers."

There in a circle of chestnut trees, a throng of doves
coo long messages in perfect alexandrines.
"La Fleur de Lys" is also there, a little café
for the far-sighted, the lazy, the critics of culture.

## IV

I came to Paris to forget you
but obstinate you absorb all my space.
You're the horrific chimera of Notre-Dame's gargoyles,
you're the angel that invincibly smiles.

Let's sign a pact (between peasant and devil):
Grant me the day to sightsee, read,
waste time, have fun, to shut you out.
Nights and dreams – I swear – are yours.

## V

The competitive search has begun. The barons of the jury
will try their hardest to deny me the French professorship.
I'm not scientific enough, it seems. Unfortunately, I lack
footnotes and glosses, critical readings and variants.

*Have you Gentlemen lived as long as I have*
*with Proust and Mallarmé, with Racine and Voltaire?*
Are they humiliating me by leaving the spirit of France
to me as passionate mistress rather than legal wife?

## VI

Traveling with too much baggage doesn't serve you well.
Some things are better off repressed,
veiled, censored, thrust into the unconscious.
A fully conscious procedure.

Example: years later you see a man you once loved,
who then was svelte and blonde, witty and kind.
For him you undress at night on the bridge of the Louvre.
But he doesn't know how often you betray him with himself.

## VII

In heaven I will find that emaciated shoot of rose
that bloomed in Mauthausen behind the shed number fourteen.
Everything capable of enduring, miraculously healed,
innocent, persistent and radiant will have those eyes.

In heaven I will find my patience and yours.
We will make a collage of missed rendezvous
and stranded sailing ships, of shreds of science,
flags drenched in tears, persistently waving.

## VIII

Patch up, repaint your past.
It's a used barge, the experts say,
pieces have fallen off, the transmission belt
is broken in three places, there's rust on the joints.

But the engine is good, eight lustra of pain
haven't mortally wounded it, and there's still fuel.
But a poet is a bit different from the others:
even if the hold is sealed, there still remains the sail.

## IX

Chalice of symbols, bliss and fidelity –
a dog is a human face immune to logic.
Like a banner, he raises up what we have lost,
periscope of scent, perception of north.

But this Norman dog Alcibiades
is imbued with other mysterious, fraternal senses.
A name is never given in vain. He shines in Socratic light,
respecting his laws, avoiding hemlock by instinct.

## X

Sunday in the country, the fretful peal of Normandy
through high branches beats unraveled time.
Falcons make their way through threads of rain,
a blue isosceles triangle mounted in a setting of black clouds.

Far away from Mediterranean troubles, the August break
invites me to string the pearls of my past backwards:
four times in love, eight books invented,
Vivaldi absorbed on certain moonlit nights.

I despise the bourgeoisie for shrinking from extremes,
trading spirit and adventure for equilibrium.
I've seen a mongrel dog worth more than a lover –
like one, but more honest, he gives back what we throw him.

## XI

The cardinal silence of the afternoon glides down,
hardening, glazing, crystallizing.
I'm an insect caught in amber,
in a thousand years we'll talk it over –

something I stole from you (or did you choose escape?)
some feather, an aura, a ray,
you're an unconscious part of me, like my clavicle or heart,
in amber we will sleep united for a thousand years or more

## XII

Music comes from every plant that grows,
the ivy is a contrabasso, the jasmine a flute,
the bluebell in the wind is a Valkyrie,
the nettle craves Aida's hunting horns.

Too much din for the dead
who died to forget life,
the deafening concert, the hostile pole
of silence, violin of God.

# XIII

*(my mother)*

From dark waves, from the bliss of nothingness
her salty welcome comes between flashing rays,
carrying baskets of wheat, nuggets of unbelievable value,
every other metaphor for the human imagination –

but where can I find words that transcend sounds,
where to dig, engrave, cast, and climb?
Scanty was my affection for you in the unconscious morning.
Blunt the weapons now of the warrior at his zenith.

# XIV

In large circles a voice arises from the lake,
the violet voice of someone who wished to die there.
This autumn is identical, but all around
gleaming dances and fires of joy.

Life interwoven with black and white:
show me the three hundred gradations
from one color to another. And make me perceive
beyond the colors from here to there.

## XV

The poet senses or tries to sense
nuances still unknown to the eye.
He uses the finest nets, invisible
to architects and salesmen.

He looks absurd; he gestures; he raves.
To take him seriously is never serious.
The acrobat looks clumsy on the tightrope
until we know he walks on an abyss.

## XVI

Leaf-laden on Norman meadows, the trees perhaps
are gigantic lances:
desperate and tenacious, they stretch up
to pierce through fog, searching for the blue –

and so our chant (curse or prayer)
rises even higher when the world
appears scant to us, a crop of faces
without a smile, not wheat but straw.

# XVII

Your gray silence, denser than music,
barely marks the wax of time.
Sea-mystery, tell your strange chronicles,
be transparent skin over the splendors of the underworld.

The gods who lived in the heavens, the Argonauts and Icarus
left no signs, that blue erases all.
But from every carefree ulysses who trusts himself to your embrace,
you strip away feather, femur, nail, or treasure.

# XVIII

The trapdoor awaits us all. Yes, all will fall through it.
But it's important to fall from on high.
To know that it was dance and war,
not waiting, sighing, grisaille.

I loved lovers of twilight too,
fishermen of shadows, the offended, the mortified.
Admirable masters, they helped me
to become their exact opposite.

# ZODIACAL SUNDAY

Where are they all going? To buy the daily paper,
to exorcise the void with Parliamentary sessions.
The intricate dynamics of a crime
keep us warm as the house cat.

I prefer the lives of saints
or rebels who set the world on fire.
Black or white, crimes they still are,
violating common sense and gray.


I don't calculate time, I feel its beat.
Seasons arrive like statues
a magic charm gives life to by a precise turn of moon.
The tides, the dance of leaves
are calls, appeals, rendezvous.

Trains and planes too pound out the rhythm
in the new heart like prophecies.
You didn't arrive by chance. You were written
on calendars printed by no one.

They told me you know that I'm here,
that you make gentle protest because I don't call.
But if I were to call you every time like clockwork,
the miracle would become *routine*.

Yes, I might look at clouds,
wasting the time that would be yours.
Softly I speak to the angel. And you know
that to angels I give one name alone.




Sunday extends its palm trees
onto the crossroads of the week.
Pigeons know it:  in dense throngs
they swarm down, undisturbed by bells.

Sunday is a strange oasis
where the soul makes sense – a bit boring, perhaps.
That's why the Moslems keep on saying
that in the end we will tire
of our harp-stringed heaven.

Hard rain for six weeks straight,
forty days of rain all together:
the deluge lasted as long.
(Nobody here at the hotel suspects anything.)

Yesterday a white dove landed
on the fourth floor terrace.
Fortunate Noah who could decipher
messages with such acumen.

Where do the wisteria of free will lead?
Am I free to raise my own hand?
Did I really choose your eyes
or follow the summons of some flute?

Be wary of flutes, the greatest of sorcerers.
They rock you and you awake inside a dream.
And caressing you, the summons seems
the brier of free will.

The morning paper alerts me:
Jupiter is favorable, but Uranus
slips a treacherous spoke
in the wheels of the triumphal chariot.

Be nice. Always give me only
the best of horoscopes. Every trip
starts off on the right foot
if no lightning is forecast.

Sagittarius promises great voyages
(but my problem is that I travel too much).
It says I inspire mad passion
but soon all madness is spent.

Sagittarius is a sheaf of arrows,
a sign of fire that promises miracles.
Do I shoot or receive those arrows?
It remains to be seen.

Slowly the hours stretch on,
each seems a hundred minutes long.
Better to have lived before Voltaire –
patron of Swiss watches.

On Sunday the hours are elastic bags
that hold everything, even a fascination for the void.
It's smart not to reject a first-time experience.
And most of all to ignore the games.


They said Cancer is a bad omen for me;
it plants the future with slowly closing traps.
But two lovers of mine are this sign.
I find that vaguely disturbing.

It would disturb me more
if it could eclipse my memory.
Whatever happens, so much goodness
has already existed.

This Sunday is over too;
the calm will soon be broken.
The will seems free. But for how long?
The stars are pure fantasy.

The ferry passes by. The last day-trippers.
Shut eyelids of shutters.
On Mondays the stars are only stars.
On Mondays I don't write poetry.

# CRISIS

*If there is a leak, do not search with a flame.*
(spontaneous hendecasyllable
from a Roman gas bill)

## Chantilly Museum

Covering the leprous nakedness of the vast walls,
between Sappho and Lorelie, the lovely tapestry unfolds.
Look, there's Icarus and Simon Magus too,
whom Peter warned not to trust in the wind.

A fine thread connects the four figures,
and I grasp it well, on the verge of a tale.
Beneath every sky, in a thousand shades of skin,
all cast atop a reef, a slippery chasm.

# *Phases*

## I

Stop! Let me off. By mistake
they've locked me in an aging body.

## II

In squalor, there is still so much life
and such a mania to see things clearly –
(but how obscurely have we pushed back
the enemy to arm the fleet)

## III

The main entrance to the house, this triumphal arch
where nightly our defeats pass by.

## IV

I felt what was once your lively champagne
turn sour and empty.
At times I had even taken it
for the wine of High Mass.

## V

I frolicked with joy; I was a three-leaf clover,
the exuberant arrogance of three beloved faces.
In February two were seized by the wind.
The last is tottering on his stem
like a tooth in an old man's mouth.

Mocking bitter emaciated autumn.

## VI

Will my sap go crazy,
pushing down instead of rising up,
turning the leaves blue,
depriving the portent of fruit?

Autumn fishermen
sometimes find treasures
when they lose faith
in what they expect.

## VII

Life is tumor and flower.
Oxygen and nitrogen.
Hell and communion.

Life is you and I, two detached stars,
in slow opposition.

## VIII

And yet I shook hands: they were sweet
knots today hard to believe.

I remember only one of the many (and I
like Adam in the Sistine Chapel).

## IX

By itself inert, alive but useless,
flexible, iron-willed, bittersweet,
in the fire of my love it was only
a moth visible
in the beacon's band of light.

## X

Messina, my deadly delight,
drop of life dripping away.
The Straits, vast bellows, forging
an unquenchable melancholy.

## XI

It would happen
if he kissed me again –
a mummy struck by gusts
of air.

## XII

The starry tiara dips,
its brilliance diminishing.
If only I could sing again the song
of the most ancient optimist – the heart:
*Bend, reed,*
*the flood must pass.*

## Future Epigraph

To your stones and your tomorrows, I entrust
the spirit, the sense, the name that was mine.

Rome, you who encircle the sacred OM of India.

## To the Readers

Free-will star is a dream hendiadys,
a pathetic longing, laughable today.
Theory, utopia, hypothesis, folly.
Neither I nor any star has ever been free.

My star is a sea forging rhythms,
reflecting caverns of a deeper yesterday.
Metaphor is a veil hiding other mysteries.
I can't see to its bottom. You are dictating to me.

## Hexaportico of Closure

You have put your life in order.
Would you give up this purposeless perfection
for a slightly imperfect purpose?

*

You who watch the water level drop
in a tub with a tiny crack.

*

This extinguishing life chars
all lovely tales of death.

*

It was not presumption but pride.
It was not humiliation but humility.

*

By accepting my cross I obliterate it.

*

I strip the Summer Garden
to adorn the Winter Palace.

# About the Title

In his *Essays on Realism,* Lukács contends that in a highly evolved capitalist society, the truly talented poet is destined to certain failure. Free will, he seems to say, like destiny, conscience, and creativity (only for the poet?) is over. It's finished for us on a practical and emotional level – even in the sense of wild abandon – after a wide spectrum of religious and secular theologies have acknowledged and often sanctioned its end in theory, embracing the dictates and liturgies of the economy and the helix of DNA.

In this book, the term *free will* is paired for antiphrastic irony with the word *star* (which represents, among cosmic phenomena, the extreme negation of freedom of choice, initiative, rhythm, movement, or direction). It is used, of course, in its simple and degraded meaning that the bourgeoisie and the proletariat have by now secularized and dried to the bone. *Platonic love* and the *Cabala* have suffered a similar fate. The term *Cabala,* from a complex text of ancient wisdom, survives here and there in everyday Italian to mean deceit, a riddle or source of lucky numbers – the dead skin of superstition crucified on the peeling walls and dusty windows of a lottery ticket shop.

# Translators' Acknowledgments

We would like to thank Maria Luisa Spaziani for her encouragement and approval of our translation and for the time she spent with us in Rome, clarifying her poetry and literary aims. Our appreciation also to Professor J. Charles Jernigan of California State University, Long Beach, and Professor Pasquale Verdicchio of the University of California, San Diego, for their invaluable comments on the translation. Finally, we would also like to thank our husbands, Greg McHolm and Michael Jones, for their patience and emotional support throughout the project.

- Cap-Saint-Ignace
- Sainte-Marie (Beauce)
Québec, Canada
1996

«L'IMPRIMEUR»